The Classical Singer's Christmas Album

Contents

On the recordings:
* Sharon Garvey, soprano
** Steven Stolen, tenor
Patrick Hansen, pianist
*** duet, with Pasquale Laurino, violin
Richard Walters, pianist for the two carols

On the cover: El Greco, *The Adoration of the Shepherds*, oil on canvas, 42 1/2 x 34 1/4 in., The Metropolitan Museum of Art

Thank you to Maria Di Palma for her suggestions for this collection.

To access companion recorded performances and piano accompaniments online, visit:
www.halleonard.com/mylibrary

Enter Code
1621-4064-0345-2316

ISBN 978-0-7935-7005-8

7777 W. Bluemound Rd. P.O. Box 13819 Milwaukee, WI 53213

Copyright © 1992 by HAL LEONARD CORPORATION
International Copyright Secured All Rights Reserved

For all works contained herein:
Unauthorized copying, arranging, adapting, recording, Internet posting, public performance, or other distribution of the printed or recorded music in this publication is an infringement of copyright.
Infringers are liable under the law.

Visit Hal Leonard Online at
www.halleonard.com

ON THE RECORDINGS

SHARON GARVEY, soprano, is a past participant in the Lyric Opera Center for American Artists at Lyric Opera of Chicago. She holds music degrees from Simpson College and Northwestern University. Ms. Garvey's opera roles include Poppea, Musetta and Micaela. She is also featured on the Hal Leonard album *Wedding Classics.*

STEVEN STOLEN, tenor, is regularly heard across the U.S. in concert and oratorio, specializing particularly in distinguished performances of Baroque music. Recent seasons have included the Britten *Serenade* with the St. Paul Chamber Orchestra, a debut with the San Francisco Symphony, and appearances with the Santa Fe Chamber Music Festival. Mr. Stolen is a frequent and acclaimed recitalist. His two dozen opera roles include Peter Quint in *The Turn of the Screw* and the title role in *Albert Herring*. He has recorded extensively for Hal Leonard, including *Popular Ballads for Classical Singers, Classical Carols, Hymn Classics,* and *Sing the Songs of Frank Loesser.*

PATRICK HANSEN, pianist, has been on the musical staff as conductor and coach at Pittsburgh Opera, Opera Memphis, Des Moines Metro Opera, and the Juilliard Opera Center. He was assistant editor for the *G. Schirmer Opera Anthology*, and is featured on other recordings released by Hal Leonard, including *Wedding Classics*, and a series of brass solos with members of The Canadian Brass. Mr. Hansen holds degrees in piano from Simpson College and the University of Missouri at Kansas City.

RICHARD WALTERS, pianist and arranger, is a composer who specializes in writing music for the voice. His principal composition studies were with Dominick Argento. He is Creative Manager of Popular, Standard and Vocal Publications at Hal Leonard. Mr. Walters is editor of many publications, including *The Singer's Musical Theatre Anthology, The Oratorio Anthology, English Songs: Renaissance to Baroque, The Singer's Movie Anthology,* and editions of the songs of Fauré, Brahms and Strauss. His concert arrangements for solo voice may be found in the collections *Classical Carols, Hymn Classics,* and *Popular Ballads for Classical Singers.*

The price of this publication includes access to companion recorded performances and piano accompaniments online, for download or streaming, using the unique code found on the title page. Visit **www.halleonard.com/mylibrary** and enter the access code.

The Classical Singer's Christmas Album

O HOLY NIGHT
(Cantique de Noël)

Adolphe Adam

Copyright © 1992 by HAL LEONARD CORPORATION
International Copyright Secured All Rights Reserved

pin - ing, Till he ap - pear'd, and the soul felt its
nel - le Et de son père ar - rê - ter le cour -
worth. A thrill of hope the
roux. Le mon - de en - tier tres -
cresc.
wear - y world re - joic - es, For yon - der breaks a
sail - le d'es - pé - ran - ce A cet - te nuit qui
cresc.
new and glo - rious morn.
lui donne un sau - veur.
f
Fall on your
Peu - - ple, à ge -
f

knees!
Oh
hear
the an - gel
noux!
At - tends
ta dé - li -
voi - ces!
O
night
di -
vran - ce.
No - ël!
No -
vine!
O
night
when Christ was
ël!
voi - ci
le Ré - demp -
born,
O
night
di -
teur,
No - ël!
No -
cresc.
cresc.

dim.
vine! O night, O night di-
ël! voi - ci le Ré-demp-
dim.
vine.
teur.
mf
Led by the
De no - tre
tr
mf
light of Faith se-rene - ly beam - ing, With glow - ing
foi que la lu-mière ar-den - te nous gui - de

hearts by his cra - dle we stand;
tous au ber- ceau de l'en - fant,
So, led by light of a star sweet - ly
comme au - tre - fois une é - toi - le bril -
gleam - ing, Here came the wise men from the O - rient
lan - te y con - dui - sit les chefs de l'o - ri -
land. The King of Kings lay
ent. Le Roi des Rois naît

cresc.
thus in low - ly man - ger, In all our trials is
dans une hum - ble crè - che; puis - sants du jour, fiers
cresc.
born to be our friend;
de vo - tre gran - deur,
f
He knows our
à vo - tre or-
f
need, to our weak - ness no
gueil c'est de là qu'un Dieu
stran - ger; Be - hold your
prê - che; cour - bez vos

King! be - fore the low - ly
fronts de - vant le Ré - demp -
bend! Be - hold your
teur, cour - bez vos
cresc.
King! your King! be - fore Him
fronts de - vant le Ré - demp -
dim.
bend!
teur.

mf
tr
Tru - ly He
Le Ré - demp-
mf
taught us to love one an - oth - er; His law is
teur a bri - sé toute en - tra - ve, La terre est
love and His Gos - pel is Peace.
li - bre et le ciel est ou - vert.
Chains shall He break, for the slave is our
Il voit un frè - re où né - tait qu'un es -

broth - er, And in His name all op-pres - sion shall
cla - ve, L'a-mour u-nit ceux qu'en-chaî - nait le
cease. Sweet hymns of joy in
fer. Qui lui di - ra no -
mf
grate - ful cho - rus raise we, Let all with - in us
tre re-con - nais-san - ce? C'est pour nous tous qu'il
cresc.
praise His Ho - ly name.
naît, qu'il souf - fre et meurt.
f
Fall on your
Peu - - ple, de -

knees! Oh hear the an - gel
bout, chan - - te ta dé - li -
voic - es! O night di -
vran - ce, No - ël! No -
vine! O night when Christ was
ël! chan - tons le Ré - demp-
born, O night di -
teur, No - ël! No -
cresc.
cresc.

vine! O night, O night di -
ël! chan - tons le Ré - demp -
vine!
teur.
f
ff
dim. e rit.
p

THE VIRGIN'S SLUMBER SONG

(Mariä Wiegenlied)

Martin Boelitz

Max Reger

Copyright © 1992 by HAL LEONARD CORPORATION
International Copyright Secured All Rights Reserved

p
Zu ih - ren Fü - ssen singt ein bun - tes Vö - ge - lein:
And soft and sweet - ly sings a bird up - on the bough:
pp
pp
Schlaf', Kind - lein, sü - sse,
Ah, ba - by, dear one,
ppp (una corda)
espress.
rit.
dolciss.
a tempo
schlaf' nun ein!
slum - ber now!
a tempo
rit.
dolciss.
espress.
p
Hold ist dein Lä - cheln, hol - der dei - nes
Hap - py is Thy laugh - ter, ho - ly is Thy
p
espress.

Schlum - mers Lust,
si - lent rest,
leg dein mü - des Köpf - chen
Lay Thy head in slum - ber,
fest an dei - ner
fond - ly on Thy
pp
Mut - ter Brust!
Moth - er's breast!
pp
Schlaf',
Ah,
Kind - lein,
ba - by,
espress.
ppp dolciss.
sü - - - sse,
dear one,
rit.
dolciss.
schlaf'
slum - ber
nun ein!
now!
a tempo
ppp

ERMUNTRE DICH, MEIN SCHWACHER GEIST
(My Weary Spirit Braces Now)

Johann Crüger (1648)

Johann Sebastian Bach

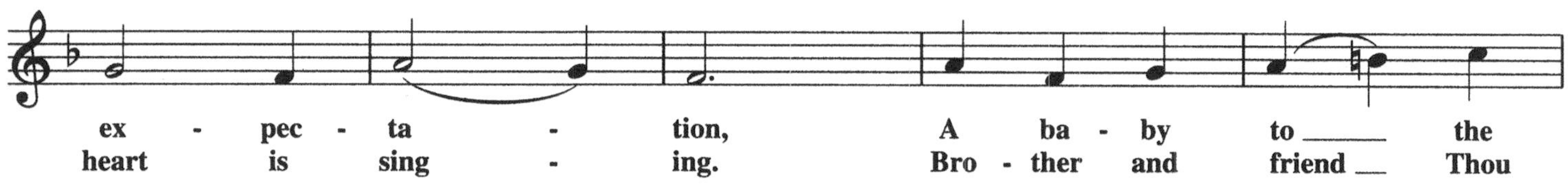

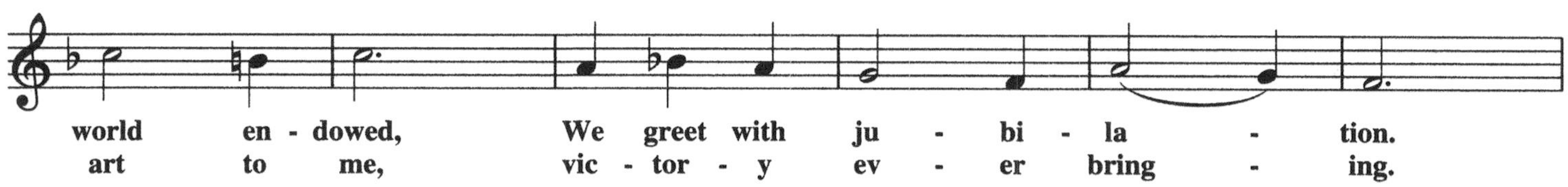

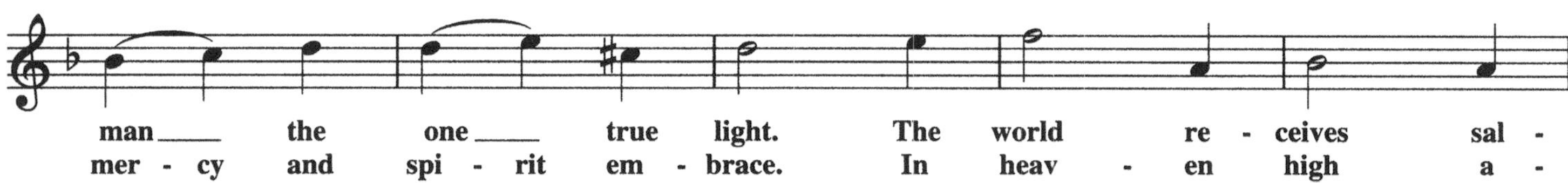

Copyright © 1992 by HAL LEONARD CORPORATION
International Copyright Secured All Rights Reserved

ERMUNTRE DICH, MEIN SCHWACHER GEIST

(My Weary Spirit Braces Now)

Johann Crüger (1648)

Johann Sebastian Bach

Copyright © 1992 by HAL LEONARD CORPORATION
International Copyright Secured All Rights Reserved

Dies ist die Nacht, dar - in es kam
Hilf, dass ich dei - ne Gü - tig - keit
und mensch - lich We - sen an sich nahm, da -
stets preis' in die - ser Gna - den - zeit und
durch die Welt mit Treu - en
mög' her - nach dort o - ben
als sei - ne Braut zu frei - en.
in E - wig - keit dich lo - ben.

O JESULEIN SÜSS

(O Jesus So Sweet)

Hall 1650

Johann Sebastian Bach

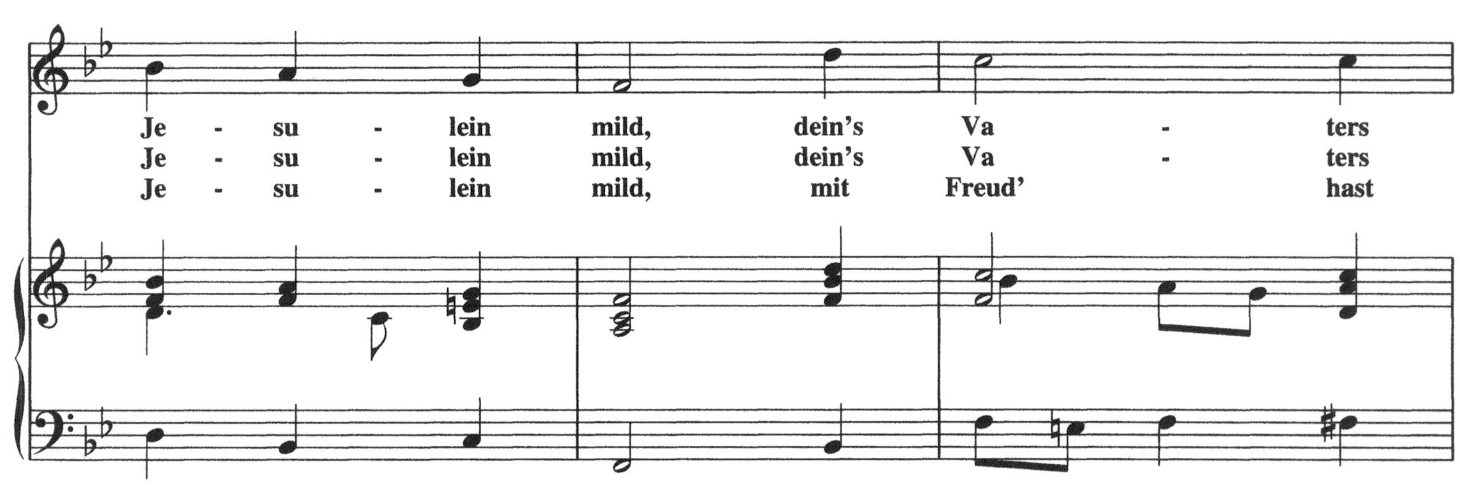

Copyright © 1992 by HAL LEONARD CORPORATION
International Copyright Secured All Rights Reserved

kom - men aus dem Him - mel -
zahlst für uns all un - sre
kommst her - ab vom Him - mels -
reich, uns ar - men Men - schen
Schuld und bringst uns in dein's
saal zu trö - sten uns im
wor - den gleich, o Je - su - lein
Va - ters Huld, o Je - su - lein
Jam - mer - tal, o Je - su - lein
süss, o Je - su - lein mild!
süss, o Je - su - lein mild!
süss, o Je - su - lein mild!

O JESULEIN SÜSS

(O Jesus So Sweet)

Hall 1650

Johann Sebastian Bach

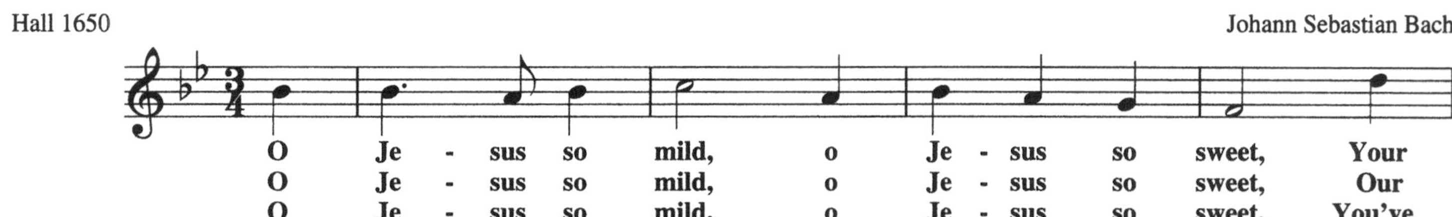

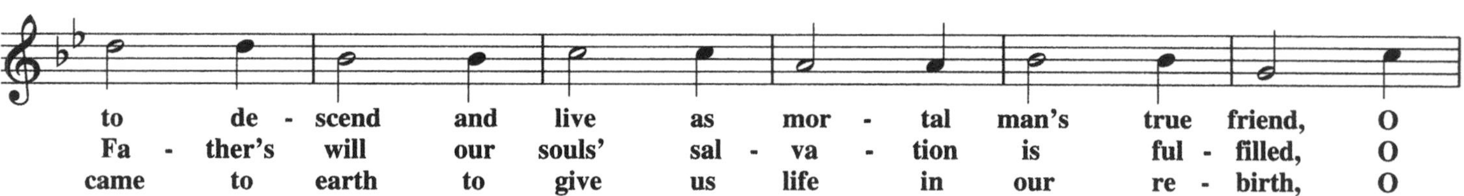

Copyright © 1992 by HAL LEONARD CORPORATION
International Copyright Secured All Rights Reserved

I STAND HERE AT THE CRADLESIDE

(Ich steh an deiner Krippe hier)

Paul Gerhard

Sigfrid Karg-Elert

Copyright © 1992 by HAL LEONARD CORPORATION
International Copyright Secured All Rights Reserved

The violin part may be carefully cut from the book.

I STAND HERE AT THE CRADLESIDE

(Ich steh an deiner Krippe hier)

Paul Gerhard

Sigfrid Karg-Elert

Copyright © 1992 by HAL LEONARD CORPORATION
International Copyright Secured All Rights Reserved

Nimm hin, nimm hin, es ist mein Geist und Sinn, Herz Seel und Mut, nimm alles hin und lass dirs wohl - ge - fal - len!
Re - ceive, re - ceive them, now I of - fer, Here my heart and soul, All I hold dear, My in - most be - ing lend Him.
f
p
f
p

Violin (ad lib.)
espressivo
mf
Voice II
mf
Ich lag in tief - ster_ To-des - nacht, du wur-dest_ mei-ne
When I lay bound_ in_ deep-est night, The gloom of_ death de-
mf sonoro
Son - ne, die_ Son - ne,_ die mir zu - ge - bracht Licht,
scend - ing, 'Twas_ You,_ dear_ Lord, who gave_ me_ light, Brought
Le - ben,_Freud und Won - ne.
life and_ joy un - end - ing.
non marcato
f
with growing expression

f
f
O Sonne, die das werte Licht des
Eternal Sun, whose own bright ray Of
sonoro
rit.
a tempo
ff
Glaubens in mir zugericht', wie schön sind deine
truth and faith can point the way: Man's pow'r cannot tran-
rfz
tr
12
Voice I f
Strahlen! Ich
scend Him! I

Voice II
f
O du fröh - li - che, o du
O thou joy - ful day, O thou
se - he dich mit Freu - den an und kann nicht satt mich
see you now with mount - ing joy, My heart can - not pos -
mf sonoro
se - li - ge, gna - den - brin - gen - de
bless - ed day; Ho - ly, peace - ful
se - hen, und weil ich nun nicht wei - ter kann, bleib
sess it. My tongue no words of praise em - ploy To

opt. 8 lower
Weih - nachts - zeit;
Christ - mas - tide.
ich an - be - tend ste - hen,
let my soul ex - press it.
Welt ging ver - lo - ren,
Earth's hopes a - wak - en,
o dass mein Sinn ein
O come, my spir - it,

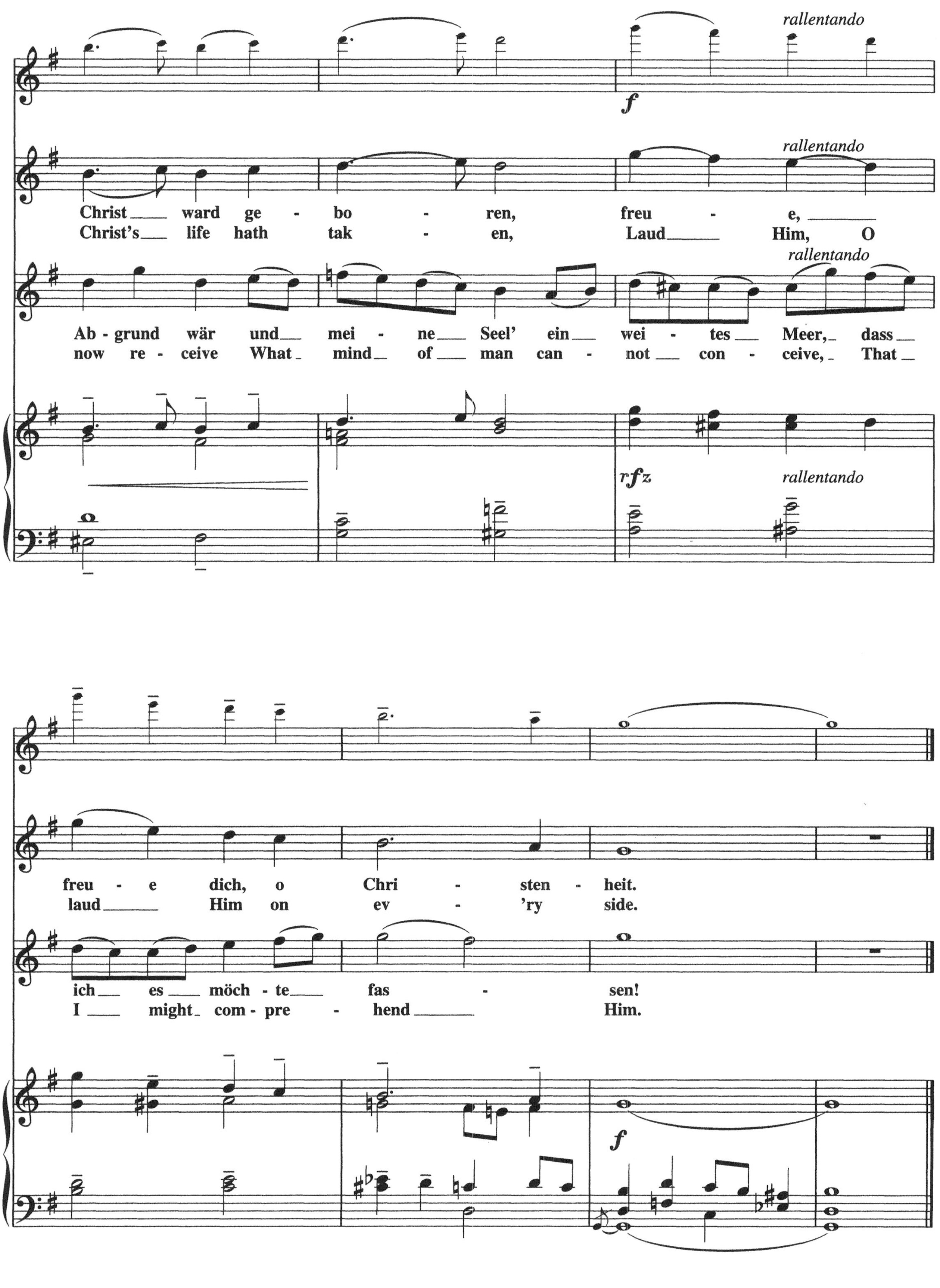

rallentando

f

rallentando

Christ ___ ward ge - bo - ren, freu - e, ___

Christ's ___ life hath tak - en, Laud ___ Him, O

rallentando

Ab - grund wär und ___ mei - ne ___ Seel' ein ___ wei - tes ___ Meer, ___ dass ___

now re - ceive What ___ mind ___ of ___ man can - not ___ con - ceive, ___ That ___

rfz rallentando

Schlafendes Jesuskind

(Gem älde von Francesco Albani)

Sohn der Jungfrau, Himmelskind!
am Boden auf dem Holz
    der Schmerzen eingeschlfaden,
Das der fromme Meister
    sinnvoll spielend,
Deinen leichten Träumen unterlegte;
Blume du, noch,
    in der Knospe dämmerned
Eingehüllt die Herrlichkeit des Vaters!
O wer sehen könnte, welche Bilder
Hinter dieser Stirne, diesen schwarzen
Wimpern sich in sanftem Wechsel malen!

The Sleeping Baby Jesus

(after a painting by Francesco Albani)

Son of the Virgin, Child of Heaven!
Asleep on the ground
    upon the wood of torture,
which the good Master,
    with effortless significance,
laid under your peaceful dreams.
You are the flower,
    even in the bud
showing the Father's glory.
O who could see what visions
behind this brow, these dark
lashes, are seen in this gentle succession.

SCHLAFENDES JESUSKIND

(The Sleeping Baby Jesus)

Eduard Friedrich Mörike

Hugo Wolf

Copyright © 1992 by HAL LEONARD CORPORATION
International Copyright Secured All Rights Reserved

leich - ten Träu-men un - ter - leg - te;
sehr ausdrucksvoll
(with great expression)
Blu - me du, noch in der Knos - pe däm - mernd ein -
- ge - hüllt die Herr - lich - keit des Va - ters!
p
sehr innig
(very fervently)
O wer se - hen könn - te, wel - che Bil - der hin - ter
mf
pp

zart
(tenderly)
die - ser Stir - ne, die - sen schwar - zen Wim - pern, sich in
pp
sanf - tem Wech - sel ma - len!
ppp
pp
wie in tiefes Sinnen verloren
(as if lost in deep thought)
pp
Sohn der Jung - frau,
ppp
Him - mels - kind!
pppp

JESUS OF NAZARETH

A. Porte

Charles Gounod

Copyright © 1992 by HAL LEONARD CORPORATION
International Copyright Secured All Rights Reserved

les ver-tus du cœur, les ver-tus du cœur.
life for-ev - er - more, life for ev - er - more.
p
mf
N'é - touf - fez
Shep - herds who
p
p
plus la voix des saints o - ra - cles; pes - ti - fé -
fold - ed your flocks be - side you, Tell what was
rés, lé - preux du la - za - reth,
told by an - gel voic - es near:
f
Es - poir en
To you this

p
Dieu, qui seul fait des mi - ra - cles. Je suis son
night is born He who will guide you Thro' paths of
dim.
pp
rit.
fils, Jé - sus de Na - za - reth!
peace to liv - ing wa - ters clear.
rit.
p a tempo
Né dans u - ne crê - che, di - vin Ré - demp - teur,
Tho' poor be the cham - ber, come here, come and a - dore;
p a tempo
i - ci - bas je prê - che, i - ci bas je prê - che
Lo! the Lord of Heav - en hath to mor - tals giv - en

les vertus du cœur.
life forever more.
mf
Plein de pitié pour la femme adultère qui s'agenouille et pleure en mon chemin,
Kings from a far land, draw near and behold Him, Led by the beam whose warning bade ye come;
Je dis à ceax qui lui
Your crowns cast down, with
p
tr
p cresc.

pp
jet - tent la pier - re, sur vo - tre
robe roy - al en - fold Him; Your King de -
pp
poco rit.
cœur a - vez - vous mis la main?
scends to earth from bright - er home.
poco rit.
pp a tempo
Né dans u - ne crê - che, di - vin Ré - demp - teur,
Tho' poor be the cham - ber, come here, come and a - dore;
pp a tempo
i - ci - bas je prê - che, i - ci - bas je prê - che
Lo! the Lord of Heav - en hath to mor - tals giv - en

les __ ver - tus du cœur.
life__ for - ev - er - more.
p
mf
A - veu - gles nés, mu -
Wind, to the ce - dars pro -
p
ets, pa - ra - ly - ti - ques, pau - vres per -
claim the joy - ful sto - ry; Wave of the
dus, boi - teux, sourds ap - pro - chez. Du
sea, the ti - dings bear a - far. The

crescendo
poco
a
Roi des Rois chan tez les saints can -
night is gone! Be hold, in all its
p
crescendo
poco
a
poco
molto
ti - ques; ou - vrez les yeuz, le - vez -
glo - ry All broad and bright ris - es th' E-
poco
molto
rit.
vous et marchez!
ter - nal morn - ing Star.
f
rit.
ff
f a tempo
Né dans u - ne crê - che, di - vin Ré - demp -
Tho' poor be the cham - ber, come here, come and a -
a tempo
f

teur,
i - ci - bas je prê - che,
dore;
Lo! the Lord of Heav - en
i - ci - bas je prê - che les ver tus du
hath to mor - tals giv - en life for - ev - er -
dim.
cœur, les ver - tus du cœur,
more, life for - ev - er - more,
p
cresc. rit.
les ver - tus du cœur.
life for - ev - er - more.
cresc. rit.
dim.
p

THE BIRTHDAY OF A KING

W. H. Neidlinger

Copyright © 1992 by HAL LEONARD CORPORATION
International Copyright Secured All Rights Reserved

ho - ly light, O'er the place where Je - sus lay: Al - le -
lu - ia! O how the an - gels sang, Al - le - lu - ia! how it
rang; And the sky was bright with a
ho - ly light, 'Twas the birth - day of a King.

'Twas a hum - ble birth-place, but
oh! how much God gave to us that day, From the
man - ger bed, what a path has led What a per - fect ho - ly

way: Al - le - lu - ia! O how the an - gels sang, Al - le -
lu - ia! how it rang; And the
sky was bright with a ho - ly light, 'Twas the
birth - day of a King.

IN THE BLEAK MIDWINTER

Christina Rossetti

Gustav Holst
Arranged by Richard Walters

Copyright © 1992 by HAL LEONARD CORPORATION
International Copyright Secured All Rights Reserved

mp
Snow had fall - en snow on snow,
Snow on
snow,
p
In the bleak mid - win - ter
Long a - go.
mp warmly
An - gels and arch - an - gels
May have gath - ered

there, Che - ru - bim and ser - a - phim
Throng - ed the air; But his moth - er
on - ly, In her maid - en bliss,
p
Wor - shipped the be - lov - ed With a
decresc.

Slower
pp tenderly, earnestly
kiss.
What can I
p
pp
give him,
Poor as I
am?
If I were a
pp
shep - herd,
I would bring a lamb;

If I were a wise man,
I would do my part;
Yet what I can I
give him:
Give
my
heart.
rit.
opt.
(,)
a tempo
mp
p
ppp
8
3

SILENT NIGHT

Joseph Mohr
English translation by John F. Young

Franz Gruber
Arranged by Richard Walters

Copyright © 1992 by HAL LEONARD CORPORATION
International Copyright Secured All Rights Reserved

hei - li - ge Paar. Hol - der Kna - be im lo - cki - gen Haar, Schlaf in
himm - lisch - er Ruh, Schlaf in himm - lisch - er Ruh.
p
Si - lent night, Ho - ly night! All is
calm, All is bright Round yon vir - gin Moth - er and

Child. Ho - ly In - fant so ten - der and mild, Sleep in
heav - en - ly peace, Sleep in heav - en - ly peace.
mp
espressivo
Si - lent night,
p
mp
espressivo

Ho - ly night,
Son of
God,
love's pure light
Ra - diant beams from
Thy ho - ly face,
espressivo
espressivo
espressivo
espressivo

With the dawn of re - deem - ing grace,
mp
p
espressivo
dolce
Je - sus, Lord, at Thy birth.
mp
p
espressivo
Je - sus,
Lord, at Thy birth.
8
pp espressivo
rit.